Matador
9 Priory Business Park
Kibworth Beauchamp
Leicestershire LE8 0RX, UK
Tel: (+44) 116 279 2299
Fax: (+44) 116 279 2277
Email: books@troubador.co.uk
Web: www.troubador.co.uk/matador

ISBN 978-1780882-475

British Library Cataloguing in Publication Data.
A catalogue record for this book is available from the British Library.

Cover Design by Staunch Design – www.staunch.com
Illustrations by Imogen McGuinness

Printed and bound in the UK by TJ International, Padstow, Cornwall

Stop

Bedwetting

in 7 days

A simple step-by-step guide to help
children conquer bedwetting problems

ALICIA EATON

Also by Alicia Eaton

FIX YOUR LIFE with NLP (Simon & Schuster) is an easy-to-read explanation of how the techniques of Neuro-linguistic Programming can help change habits and behaviours. Chapters include: Fix your Weight; Fix your Habits and Motivation; Fix your Fears & Phobias; Fix your Confidence; Fix your Health & Wellbeing.

A range of CDs is also available:

- Relax Now

- Boost Your Confidence

- Weight Off Your Mind

- The Hypnotic Gastric Band

- Garden of Your Life (Meditation)

- Dry Beds Now (Age 5 -10)

- Stop Bedwetting Now (Age 5 – teens)

- A Magic Day Out (Age 5-12)

Please see website: www.aliciaeaton.co.uk for full details

ABOUT THE AUTHOR

Alicia Eaton is a fully qualified Clinical Hypnotherapist and is also Licensed by The Society of NLP as a Master Practitioner of Neuro-Linguistic Programming and an Advanced Therapeutic Specialist. She has been trained by the industry's experts - Richard Bandler (co-creator of NLP) and Paul McKenna.

She has been part of Paul McKenna's seminar assisting team for many years and also fine-tuned her coaching skills with Michael Neill, the renowned success coach.

As well as working with adults, she is now a recognised expert on the use of NLP and hypnosis with children and runs successful practices in both London's Harley Street and Hertfordshire.

A qualified Montessori Teacher, she was Principal of her own school for five years and went on to study Developmental Psychology at The Anna Freud Centre and University College London, before undergoing her Hypnotherapy training.

She lives in Hertfordshire and has three children.

"Alicia Eaton has a real gift for communicating complex ideas in a way that makes them easy to incorporate into your daily routine. I highly recommend her work, particularly when applied to children (and their parents!)"

Michael Neil bestselling author of 'You Can Have What You Want' and ''Supercoach'

"What a wonderful, practical, easy-to-read book. Alicia's common-sense approach, skills and experience – plus a liberal sprinkling of NLP techniques makes this a must-read book for parents.

Dr. Stephen Simpson MB CHB MFOM MBA
NLP Trainer

"Stop Bedwetting in 7 days is a very good book. I have found it to be clear, effective and have recommended it to a number of my patients.

Dr.Anne Wright – Consultant Paediatrician
Evelina Children's Hospital, Guys & St.Thomas NHS Trust

This is a must-have for parents struggling to handle bedwetting. This great book is bursting with practical advice and simple ideas that really work.

Sue Atkins – 'The Parenting Expert'
Author of 'Raising Happy Children for Dummies'

CONTENTS

INTRODUCTION

Let me start by being honest with you.......

When this book was first published in September 2009, I could not be 100% certain that the techniques that I had been using successfully for many years with my clients, would easily translate into a system for parents to use with their own children.

But my frustration at seeing growing numbers of children (through no fault of their own) locked in a repetitive pattern of bedwetting, fuelled me on to at least *try* to pass the message on. My gut instincts were that bedwetting is not a problem that children simply have to put up with, until 'they grow out of it', as so many of the experts would have us believe – there are solutions.

'Stop Bedwetting' was launched in September 2009 with an interview on BBC Radio 4's Woman's Hour and the response, whilst positive, was also one of scepticism. Is hypnotherapy really safe to use with children? Could it be possible to solve a problem as difficult as bedwetting, through a simple book? And wasn't I somehow being unprofessional in offering parents 'hope', when we all know that in fact no-one can solve this problem and you just have to sit it out?

Well, I am pleased to report that over two years of research and results, can now speak for itself. Sales of this book now run into the thousands and children from all parts of the world have successfully fixed their bedwetting habits by using it.

Each day I receive emails from grateful parents not only in the UK, but also the United States, Canada, Australia, New Zealand, Hong Kong, South America, all parts of Europe and Scandinavia.

I'm now regularly asked to train other Practitioners in my methods and hypnotherapists as far away as India, are adopting my system for use with their own clients.

My own survey in which 165 parents took part, (results on page 45) showed that over 70% of children achieved dry nights following this system and 85% of parents would recommend this system to others.

I've now used all the feedback that I've received from parents and children and updated the 'Stop Bedwetting' system to make it better than ever before.

And, I'm delighted to be able to say that so many more people – parents, GPs, Consultant Paediatricians - are now acknowledging the value of using a behavioural approach such as this one, to solve bedwetting, rather than resorting to the use of medication and drugs as has been the case for many years.

My system incorporates the latest techniques and success strategies from the fields of hypnotherapy and NLP (Neuro-linguistic Programming). People are often surprised when I tell them that I regularly see children for hypnotherapy sessions, for whilst we're used to hearing about hypnotherapy helping adults quit smoking or lose weight, it's less well known that these same techniques can be used very safely and effectively with children.

These techniques complement a child's natural development and encourage those vital mind and body connections to be made. Once these are established, there's no looking back – you'll have dry nights forever.

I've been able to develop this system as a result of being trained by three of the world's experts in the field of 'success and changework'. Collectively, Richard Bandler (the co-creator of NLP), Paul McKenna and Michael Neill have enabled thousands of people to change their lives for the better. I've worked alongside them since 2004 and studied their methods in detail.

In this book, I'm going to show you how easy it can be to apply the very same techniques and success strategies to this widespread and common childhood problem. In just a week, you'll have mastered some of the techniques that will enable you to enjoy the life-changing benefits that achieving night-time dryness will have on you and your family.

Changes will be noticeable in days and the benefits will be felt for years.

CHAPTER ONE

•

Bedwetting – what's it all about?

BEDWETTING – WHAT'S IT ALL ABOUT?

If you have a child that wets the bed, you might be feeling as if you are the only parent in the world whose child has this unwanted habit. It can be difficult to discuss the subject with family and friends, leaving you at a loss to understand why your child has failed to stop a habit that so many other children seem to get over with ease.

If this sounds familiar, then take comfort from knowing that more than 750,000 children in the UK accidentally wet their beds at night. Bedwetting still occurs on most nights in 15% of all five year olds and is still a problem for 3% of all 15 year olds. The numbers are just an estimate, of course, because bedwetting is not a subject that parents are happy to discuss openly. In many cases, it isn't even a subject that is talked about within the family.

The truth is that millions of children from all over the world, wet their beds or have to rely on protective pants every single night. If your child is one of them, is very likely that there are at least one or two more in their class at school with the same problem.

You are not on your own and the good news is that bedwetting can be overcome.

For a number of years, I have been helping parents and their children to conquer this habit. I have seen the consequences of bedwetting – children suffer from a lack of confidence and low self-esteem, often failing to reach their full potential. Invitations to sleep overs with other children have to be refused; school trips and camps are met with fear and family holidays are the not the relaxing times they are meant to be.

Let me put your mind at ease by reassuring you that bedwetting can be cured and the positive effects on your child will be amazing. Solving your child's bedwetting problem is much more than just achieving night time dryness – it is about giving your child an increase in their level of self-confidence both at home and at school, which can lead to improved performance in the classroom and better interaction with their peers.

My reason for writing this book is that I believe the process I have successfully developed over a number of years, can be easily learned by parents.

In order to solve problems, we often need to *stop* things happening. And the best way to do this is to *think* carefully about what you do want to happen and then *plan* how to be successful.

With this book, I've done the work for you and devised a plan that will enable you and your child to achieve that success. The effects on your child once they've got rid of the bedwetting habit will be life-changing. The effects on you, as a parent, will be equally liberating and rejuvenating!

Before we look at how hypnotherapy and NLP could help you and your child, let's have a look in more detail at what this problem is all about.

Bedwetting – also known as nocturnal enuresis – affects most children up to the age of three as the development of bladder function control can be a slow process. Bedwetting can continue to be quite common in children up the age of eight and sometimes even into their teenage years.

Studies show that bedwetting children who are given professional help and advice are more likely to become dry than those who aren't. With one or two children in every 100 failing to achieve night time dryness, it is vitally important to get help at the right time. Some children never quite 'grow out' of their bedwetting habit, often carrying the scars into adulthood. Prolonged childhood bedwetting can manifest itself in many ways: difficulties forming relationships and getting jobs, susceptibility to stress, anxiety and even depression.

HOW COMMON IS BEDWETTING?

Bedwetting is a common problem, especially in the under-fives. According to figures published by the British Medical Journal, at the age of five as many as 20 children in 100 will have difficulty in controlling their bladders at night-time.

By age seven, this figure has dropped to around eight children in every 100, so we can see that most children will develop that vital mind/body link at around the age of six years.

It's at this age that children enter a new developmental phase. A good indicator of this happening is the loss of milk teeth. If your child still wets the bed at night and is starting to lose teeth, I'd recommend introducing this system – it shows it's the right time and will support their natural development.

The research goes on to show that by age 10, there are still 5 children in every 100 experiencing problems. So, not much progress is made with children who are left waiting for nature to take its' course.

POSSIBLE CAUSES

You may hear many reasons being put forward as possible causes of a bedwetting problem such as:

- the size of the bladder

- a urinary tract infection

- lack of hormones to concentrate urine

- something that runs in families

- stress or anxiety

Some children are referred to Enuresis Clinics by their GPs and, as a first step in the process, it is sensible to rule out the possibility of any infection which can easily be treated with antibiotics, or to identify the possibility of some other physiological cause for the problem.

Once it's been established that these possibilities do not play a part, the clinic will often suggest solutions such as using alarms in the bed, which will wake the child once wetness is detected.

If alarms are not successful, children may be prescribed medication or drugs to concentrate their urine and even in extreme cases, will be offered anti-depressants.

Our bodies release a hormone whilst we sleep called vasopressin and this concentrates our urine. When children struggle to control their bladders at night, it's often assumed that an absence of the hormone is the cause of this. Doctors however, do tell me that there is no definitive test to check whether this is the case in each particular child and so the use of a drug called Desmopressin - a synthetic hormone that mimics the action of the real hormone – is really a 'best guess'.

It should solve the problem pretty much immediately, if it's going to work at all, but I have come across children who have been taking it for many months and some even for years, without achieving dry nights – it's still a hit and miss affair. After this time, it's very likely that it's not going to work at all and if your child is in this situation, I would recommend a return visit to the practitioner who prescribed it for you, with a view to stopping it altogether.

I believe the solution to this problem has to come 'from within' rather than from some sort of external crutch.

Just like a smoker who quits cigarettes with the aid of nicotine replacement gum, or an overweight person who loses weight by drinking diet shakes, instead of eating proper food, the problem may appear to have been solved, but quickly returns once the crutch is taken away.

Only changes made on the 'inside' can be guaranteed to produce long-lasting results on the 'outside'.

Of course, some children will achieve success with the help of an alarm or the use of medication, but I'm more concerned about the ones who don't. Too many revert to old habits within a short period and, in extreme cases, can continue to wear protective pull-up pants at night until they are teenagers.

Most children do eventually grow out of the bedwetting habit, but a small proportion will remain stuck in this cycle of behaviour and continue to wet the bed throughout their adult life. Without breaking this pattern of behaviour, the eventual effects are all too obvious.

EMOTIONAL CAUSES

In a minority of cases, there can be a sudden onset of bedwetting. If your child has been dry at night for several months or even years and starts having wet beds again, this can be caused by an emotional upset such as a change at home or stress with school work. This is usually temporary and not the same as an ongoing bedwetting problem. Most parents know their children and will be able to tell the difference, so if your gut feeling is that there is no real explanation for the bedwetting – go with your instincts but monitor the situation closely.

Neuro-psychologists now agree that there's a complex co-ordination that needs to take place between the nerves and the muscles of the bladder and more often than not, a delay in this happening is what holds children back.

New neural pathways or connections are needed to be made in the brain, in order to achieve night-time dryness and I'm going to show you how easy it can be to speed this process up.

CHAPTER 2

•

Understanding habits and behaviours

GETTING INTO THE HABIT

In the overwhelming majority of bedwetting cases, the cause is simply *habit*. Somehow over the years, your child got into a habit of wearing pull-up pants or similar absorbent protection and just never learnt how to stay dry all night. It's as simple as that.

And then you found yourselves caught in that 'catch 22' situation. Never quite confident enough to stop using absorbent pants (after all, think about the embarrassment an accident would cause if you were staying in a hotel) –but at the same time never quite giving your child's mind the opportunity to allow the neurological pathways to wire themselves up and create that 'auto-pilot'.

It's a common enough problem and in fact, it's the reason why more and more children are beginning to suffer from night-time bedwetting problems than ever before. Have you noticed how the supermarket shelves are increasingly stocking night-time 'pull-up' protective pants for teenagers up to the age of 15?

A decade or so ago these just did not exist to the same extent. Make no mistake, the manufacturers are more than happy to keep on making these in all sorts of fancy designs and colours to keep your child happy.

But I believe, these may well be the cause of the problem, rather than a solution.

A quick survey of my bedwetting clients revealed that the average amount of money spent on protective night-time pants is £7 - £10 per week. Wow, just think how good you're going to feel when all that money can stay in your purse, rather than being thrown in the bin (quite literally!). And I wonder what you'll be spending it on........

PAST GENERATIONS

Quite a few of the bedwetting problems parents encounter today are as a result of lifestyle changes that have taken place in our society and the changes in our toilet training methods in general.

It's not uncommon nowadays to hear grandparents proudly announce that they never had problems toilet-training their young babies. And according to some - like my own mother – it was all over and done with by the age of 12 months! Of course, today's mums will roll their eyes up to the ceiling and take this piece of information with a pinch of salt.

But back in the days before disposable nappies had been invented, the incentive to get your baby dry and out of nappies was very much greater. Changing terry cloth nappies was hard work with hours of cleaning, boiling, sterilising and washing on a daily basis. Being a 'stay-at-home' mum was not so much a lifestyle choice but more of a necessity – someone had to do it.

And 'staying at home' also meant staying in one place for most of the day – making it very much easier to build up a routine for toilet training. Modern day mums are much more likely to be working outside the home, resulting in young children being ferried to and from nurseries or childminders.

Even our shopping habits have changed - most of us can spend several hours on a large supermarket visit rather than a quick 20 minute daily trip to the local shops, as was often the case years ago. Nowadays, it's a brave mother who's willing to chance her luck doing the shopping with a toddler in the throes of toilet-training. All this moving around, usually by car, makes dealing with 'accidents' that much harder.

Today's children have busy social lives and many start having sleepovers with friends at a much earlier age than they used to. So it's only natural that we do everything we possibly can to avoid those embarrassing accidents and encourage our children to continue wearing nappies or pull-ups for much longer.

The nappy manufacturers have done everything they can think of to make our lives easier and over the years they've improved the quality, fit and design to such an extent that your child no longer needs to even feel wet when they urinate. How comfortable can life get?

It's no wonder toilet training can become a bit of an uphill struggle for many parents – let's face it, life has to get a lot worse before it gets any better. Is there ever a good time to take off those nappies?

THE TRUE VALUE OF AN ACCIDENT

Avoiding accidents can mean missing out on valuable learning opportunities. Babies growing up in pre-disposable nappy days very quickly made a connection between urinating and feeling wet. Once this link was established, a second one was made – a relaxing of the bladder muscles and the release of urine.

And once you learn how to start something, you can quickly learn how to stop it. Constant repetition of a piece of behaviour – literally, your child weeing over and over again throughout the day – is what allows that vital mind / body connection to become more established. Having these experiences enables your child's mind to begin understanding changing behaviour.

Knowing this, it becomes easier to see why so many more children nowadays are struggling to master the art of bladder control. Not only are they missing out on the valuable learning opportunities that numerous toilet accidents throughout the day would have given them, but they're also missing out on the experience of feeling wet as the quality of nappies or pull-ups improves.

Our brains can be likened to a piece of plastic that moulds and adapts to fit the experiences in our environment. If your child never experiences the feeling of wetness when releasing urine from the bladder, those valuable connections in the brain cannot be made.

Of course, eventually all children will become toilet trained during the day – it just happens a little later nowadays than it used to. Getting dry at night then becomes the next hurdle to cross and many parents get stuck here – not knowing quite how to make this happen.

SELF-IMAGE

Your child's self-image plays a crucial role in literally predicting whether or not your child will be successful. Once the idea of being a bedwetter has established itself in your child's mind, it becomes a lot harder to change the pattern of behaviour.

Our behaviours will always match the image we have of ourselves and in this book, I'll be showing you how to ensure your child develops a positive self- image making success that much easier to achieve.

As scientists begin to discover and understand more about how our brains function, it's becoming increasingly clear that the best treatment for bedwetting is following a programme that encourages the child's mind to do one of two things:

either

get up when receiving a signal from the bladder and go to the bathroom

or

stay asleep all night and hold on till the morning.

I've devised this easy-to-read guide with activities and strategies for you and your child to follow over the course of 7 days to enable those vital connections to be established more quickly. We're going to speed up the body's natural processes.

The chances are that sooner or later, those vital connections will end up being made anyway – but why wait till your child is yet another year older? How many more sleepovers and school trips will be missed? How many more embarrassing moments will there be? And how much more washing will you tolerate? With this system you'll be able to help your child beat this habit once and for all.

It is possible to get through all the exercises in this programme in less than 7 days – some children who come to see me for a face-to-face appointment can be dry on the first night after just the initial session. However, it's not easy to predict how quickly your child's mind and body will start to synchronise which is why I suggest taking a full 7 days to give your child's brain valuable thinking time. And if you feel your child could do with some extra time to fully understand all the techniques, then it is possible to extend this programme for up to 14 days. However, do make sure your child gets daily practice, for repetition, repetition, repetition is the key to success.

CREATING AN AUTO-PILOT

Conscious thinking uses different parts of the brain to unconscious learning so it's best to allow time for your child's brain to activate a deeper, more permanent intelligence.

After all, you're going to be asking your child to do things when they're half-asleep – in other words, not very conscious at all! The more deeply we can embed new patterns of behaviour on their subconscious minds, the easier it will be for them to operate on 'auto-pilot'.

Have you ever driven a car on a long journey and got to your destination unable to remember much about the driving part of it? That's because your conscious mind switched off for a while and started thinking about other things. Fortunately, the ability to drive has been imprinted on your subconscious mind – remember all those driving lessons you took? So your subconscious mind was able to take over and do the job for you – your very own automatic pilot.

And you're going to be able to do exactly the same for your child – creating an automatic pilot that can register signals from the bladder, wake him up and steer him in the direction of the bathroom in the middle of the night. It's easier than you think.

CHAPTER THREE

Bedwetting, Hypnotherapy & NLP – a different solution to a familiar problem

WHAT'S THE BEST WAY TO STOP MY CHILD'S BEDWETTING HABIT?

Because of the stigma attached to bedwetting, most people start their search for help through the internet. Put "bedwetting" into any internet search engine and you will be given a number of different treatment options ranging from the use of electronic alarms,, medication to concentrate the flow of urine or even anti-depressants.

I know that each of these methods have differing levels of success and some parents will say that the alarms or medication have worked for their child. I can only say that in my experience of helping children with a bedwetting condition, these methods often only manage the problem in the short term rather than cure it for good and around 70% of children will go back to their old habits and behaviours after 2-3 months.I helped one couple that had tried three different alarms, each of which had terrified their child before they consulted their family doctor who prescribed medication to reduce the flow of urine. This process went on for nearly two years before they brought their child to see me. Two years – that's a lot of wet sheets and pyjamas!!

WHAT'S THE ALTERNATIVE?

I believe the key to ending bedwetting once and for all is to encourage your child's mind and body to work more closely together. Children's minds are continually creating new connections called neural pathways, to accommodate new patterns of thinking and behaviour.

In my Hypnotherapy and NLP (Neuro-Linguistic Programming) practice, I've been seeing children with bedwetting problems regularly since 2004. I believe I have developed a quicker, safer and more natural alternative to changing night time habits for good. It doesn't involve any gadgets nor giving a child drugs - which has to be a good thing.

Over the years, I noticed that the majority of children who came to see me for a face-to-face session were dry that same night. Keeping dry however, often proved much harder which is why I started giving visualisation exercises as homework and a CD to listen to as back up. The repetition of visualisation work produced far better results and was the reason for my packaging it up as this book. It isn't always instant success and there may be several wet nights in the first couple of weeks but over a period of 3-4

weeks, a pattern of dry nights usually starts to
establish itself.

HYPNOTHERAPY & NLP – IT'S CHILD PLAY

Whilst consulting a hypnotherapist may not be the solution that is uppermost in your mind to begin with, it is now becoming more widely accepted throughout the medical profession and many parents are referred to me by their family clinic and GP.

If the idea of hypnotising and reprogramming children's minds sounds a bit strange – fear not. During this stage of life, children's minds are like sponges absorbing all sorts of information naturally. In other words, they are being hypnotised all the time. You only have to observe a child's ability to gaze at the TV and recite the jingles back perfectly to see this in action.

That 'deeply relaxed state' is what we try to re-create during a session because, as you will have already witnessed when your child watches TV, information can be absorbed more deeply. In this instance, the information will be all about having dry beds forever.

Neuro-linguistic Programming, despite its' complicated name is really quite simple. NLP helps us to deal with what we think, what we say and what we do by breaking down our thought patterns and changing them for the better. Our thinking has a direct impact on our feelings and our behaviour.

Remember, your child's mind is being moulded and shaped by their environment all the time. In fact, your child spends many moments in a trance-like state every day, randomly absorbing all the messages around him. Some of these messages are good ones such as being praised for producing a good piece of homework - and others are not so helpful, such as having accidents and wetting the bed. Children quickly build up a picture of things they do well and things they do less well – and then go on to behave accordingly.

Techniques such as hypnotherapy and NLP are, in my opinion, under-utilised in the treatment of children but more parents are now turning to them as traditional methods fail to help their children.

As a result of the general lack of understanding about how these methods work, we are still more likely to prescribe unnecessary drugs and medication for our children, such as general anaesthetics to overcome dental phobias and drugs to reduce the flow of urine, rather than consider safer, more natural alternatives.

RESULTS OF MY SURVEY

After this book had been available for 6 months, I carried out a survey by sending out emails asking a variety of questions. 165 people replied and here is a summary of the results:

The age range varied from 4 years old to 14 years, so I have broken some of the results down by age group.

Overall, an overwhelming 85% of respondents said they would recommend this system to other parents. The results went on to show that 73% of children did achieve dry nights using the system.

For 58% of children this was 3 or more dry nights each week, compared to only 13% who were achieving this before carrying out the 7 day programme.

And for 30%, this was total dryness after following the 7 day programme, compared to zero at the start.

I looked more closely at the group of children who had **never** had any dry nights before in their lives and the results following the programme, were as follows:

Age	Percentage achieving dry nights
4	75.0
5	90.0
6	64.5
7	62.5
8	28.7
9	42.8
10	41.8
11	20.0
12	37.5
13	20.0
14	100 (Note: just one respondent)

Not surprisingly, the figures for the younger age group were higher – leaving me to feel that just like learning how to swim, speak a foreign language or play a musical instrument, it's best to follow this type of programme as early as possible to avoid the wrong habits becoming deeply ingrained.

However, when I asked how many children who had already experienced **some** dry nights (but simply not enough) could see a marked improvement following the programme, the figures were much higher in the older age groups.

Age	Percentage achieving dry nights
4	50
5	50
6	61
7	79
8	66
9	86
10	83
11	90
12	88
13	60
14	50

These results reflect the outcome after following the 7 day programme with reinforcement from listening to the audio programme and repetition of the visualisation exercises. Over the following months, these children can expect their results to continue improving till they reach 100% dryness.

There are a number of factors that can affect these results. As well as the age and psychological makeup of each child, there is also medical history and the parent's own relationship with the child plus their personal interpretation of the programme, to be taken into consideration.

As parents we all know how much easier it is for an 'outsider' such as a teacher or tutor to sit and work with our children, than it is for us. And I also appreciate that not every parent will be able to deliver the NLP techniques in the way that I can, following all my years of training.

However, following these positive results, I would very much hope that GPs, Health Visitors and Enuresis Clinics consider adopting these methods, training their staff and using them as a first resort, rather than recommending them as a last resort, which is often what happens. Not only will our children be healthier and happier but both parents and hospitals will save an enormous amount of money.

THE NORWEGIAN STUDY

In 2004, a study appeared in The Journal of the Norwegian Medical Association about using hypnotherapy to treat patients with chronic nocturnal enuresis. This study consisted of 12 boys ranging in age from 8 to 16.

All the boys had been diagnosed with primary nocturnal enuresis and four were also diagnosed with diurnal enuresis (daytime accidental urination). All 12 participants reported an average of 0 dry nights per week. The 12 participants also had a family history of bedwetting and had tried other forms of treatment such as bedwetting alarms and medication.

The boys had between 2 and 8 hypnotherapy sessions as part of the study and also practised self-hypnosis for one month after the sessions.

Two follow-ups were performed at 3 months and one year intervals. During both follow-ups, 9 out of the 12 participants reported 7 out of 7 dry nights per week. The researchers referred the 3 patients who continued to experience bedwetting to seek additional medical treatment.

The researchers concluded that hypnotherapy is an effective treatment for children diagnosed with nocturnal enuresis.

Source: Diseth, T.H. & Vandick, I.H. (2004)

CHAPTER FOUR

•

Getting started – how to use this book

HOW TO USE THIS BOOK

This book is for you and your child to use together. But, I do recommend that you read the book from start to finish *before* beginning to use this system with your child. You'll have a better idea of what's involved and how to implement it into your daily lives.

Before beginning, you'll need to discuss the plan of action with your child in detail explaining that soon they'll be free of this miserable habit – the embarrassment and wet beds.

Traditionally, we've been led to believe that it's better not to discuss bedwetting with our children for fear of upsetting them. In my experience, this is now producing a generation of parents and children who have never acknowledged that it's an unwanted pattern of behaviour. It's easy to move from wearing nappies to night time pull-ups without so much as a by or leave. The habit is hushed up and it's quite common for other family members not to even be aware of it.

One mother contacted me after purchasing this book and told me that her eight year old daughter was instantly dry at night after the conversation they'd had at the start of this programme. It transpired that her daughter simply hadn't realised that other children no longer wear pull-ups at night and that she should be using the bathroom instead. She was easily able to take control of her bladder and asked her mother why she hadn't said anything sooner!

So, the conversation you'll be having with your child at the start of this programme is a vital part of sowing those seeds of success.

You'll need to get your child's agreement by asking questions such as 'Does that sound ok to you?' or 'Are we going to do that?' as you outline how the programme will work and the commitment that will be required to following daily exercises.

It's possible to work through this book very quickly, but I'm going to advise that you take at least 7 days to allow your child's understanding to deepen. Mark a date on the calendar to indicate the day you will finally rid yourselves of this habit and begin a new life. Better still, get a roll of old wallpaper and stick a large piece of it on your child's bedroom wall – this will give you a blank canvas on which to create a daily diary. Can you think of a date in the future, say a holiday in a couple of months' time, when your child would really want to be dry by? It's good to have an incentive and a key date to be working towards.

(If you prefer you can take up to 14 days to work through all the exercises, but make sure your child is doing at least one activity every day.)

GETTING STARTED

The activities that I've devised are a combination of listening, drawing and visualising. They all serve the same purpose and that is for you and your child to begin creating better pictures in your minds, as this will turn things around for you.

Up until now, your minds have been filled with images of wet sheets, extra laundry, embarrassment and feelings of failure. You probably both have a very good idea of how you don't want things to be and after a while it can become a lot harder to imagine a positive future. These activities are going to make it easier for you.

Having good pictures in our minds is an important step towards achieving success, for human beings are naturally drawn to the ideas in their minds. If the only thoughts and pictures your child has are of wet beds and failures, it's going to be a lot harder to achieve night-time dryness.

HYPNOTIC RECORDING

The first thing you will need to do is to DOWNLOAD a special recording called 'Dry Beds Now' from my website: www.stopbedwettingin7days.co.uk. This is available **free of charge** and your child will need to listen to this on a daily basis for at least a week. He'll need to start listening to this from Day 5 – so get prepared and download it onto an iPod or computer as soon as possible.

Just 20 minutes long, this recording is filled with positive suggestions and visualisation exercises to help prepare your child's mind to be receptive to the idea of controlling his or her bladder at night without having to rely upon protective pants. It's best to provide a quiet time and place without interruptions at some point during the day for your child to do this.

If you prefer to have the recording on a CD, it's possible to purchase one of these through the website. Other CDs available from the website are 'Stop Bedwetting Now' (suitable for all ages including teenagers) and 'A Magic Day Out' – a confidence boosting story for up to age 12. It can be useful to have these additional CDs to keep the momentum of the programme going and provide variety for your child – see further details at www.aliciaeaton.co.uk.

Your child can listen to these once he is in bed at night, but during the first couple of days, it's good to include some 'daytime' listening too. But please, DO NOT play any of the CDs whilst you are driving in the car or operating machinery – they're very relaxing and will encourage you to close your eyes!!

DRAWING ACTIVITIES

Some of the activities require your child to draw pictures - ensure you have a pad of A4 paper and some felt-tipped pens to hand. I have created some spaces within the book for these, but your child may wish to do some additional drawing. These drawing activities will help with that process of creating good ideas in your child's mind.

The activities should be preceded by a discussion between yourself and your child, so set aside 10-15 minutes for this. During a conversation, you'll be able to get your child thinking on the right track leaving them to complete the picture afterwards. Encourage your child to tell you about the picture in as many details as possible – this will ensure that positive ideas are cementing themselves in their minds.

If your child is older or a teenager, they may prefer to make notes or write their thoughts down in sentences, rather than draw pictures. This will work equally well, for it's the pictures that are being triggered off inside their minds by the drawing or writing activity, that are the most important ones here.

EYES CLOSED / VISUALISATION ACTIVITIES

Other activities are visualisation techniques that are quite literally, eyes closed imagination games for you to guide your child through. Although fairly simple to do, they have a wonderful effect on helping people achieve their goals. And again, if your child is a teenager then please do reassure them that these types of activities are exactly the same as those done by adults using NLP techniques.

It's best to set aside around 15-20 minutes for these and pick a time when you're unlikely to be interrupted.

Providing your child isn't too sleepy, incorporating these activities into your bedtime routine can be ideal.

KEEPING GOOD PICTURES IN MIND

Human beings are naturally goal-seeking and when I work with clients on self-improvement, one of the most important things I can tell them is "What you see, is what you get". As we think and speak, our minds are constantly making pictures, even if you're not aware of it. All throughout the day, your mind is doing this, whether you're thinking about phoning a friend, what to make for supper or what time you need to collect the children from school – little pictures will keep flashing through your mind.

We are magnetically drawn towards getting what we see and as with the drawing or writing activities, the visualisation exercises will encourage your child's mind to focus on what they do want, rather than on what they don't want. As I've said before, it doesn't matter how badly you and your child want dry beds – if he or she can't imagine themselves in the future no longer needing to wear pants at night-time, they are not going to be able to do it.

These techniques are just like the ones used by top athletes and sports people. They know the difference these can make to their performance. But they take the whole process one step further and 'mentally rehearse' themselves being even more successful if they want to improve and really become a winner. Runners see themselves running even faster, footballers see themselves scoring goal after goal. Your body cannot tell the difference between a vividly imagined experience and one that really happened.

Now you might be thinking to yourself – 'oh come on, of course I can tell the difference between an imagined experience and one that happened for real. But think back to the last time you saw a scary movie at the cinema. Whilst your mind knew that what you were watching was only a movie, your body nevertheless responded as if it were happening for real. Your heart may have started to beat a little faster, your breathing became a little shallower, your hands might have begun to feel sweaty and some of you will even have screamed out loud! Whilst you *know* that what you were watching wasn't happening for real, your body nevertheless did *feel* as if it was.

And in just the same way, we're going to be guiding your child through a series of exercises that will enable his or her body to literally feel as if it does have full control over the bladder.

Studies show that this kind of 'rehearsal' really does have a positive effect on the outcome. All sorts of magical wiring up takes place in the brain as you practise a scenario over and over and your child is going to have the opportunity to allow this to happen to them.

WHAT TO EXPECT

This bedwetting system has now been used by thousands of children all around the world – so there's plenty of evidence to suggest what is likely to happen once you have followed the 7 day programme.

A small *minority* of you will have instant success – just like that mother of the eight year old daughter I told you about.

An even smaller *minority* will have no success whatsoever – there are many possible reasons for a lack of success rather than a simple failure of this system and I will go into more detail about these later.

The overwhelming *majority* of you however, will get some dry nights in the first week and this will gradually increase over the following two to three weeks. This is usually followed by a period of stabilisation – not every night may yet be dry, but a pattern of dry nights begins to build up as your child's confidence grows.

It's going to be important to view any wet nights as 'one-off accidents' and not an indication that the system is not working. As already mentioned, these accidents provide valuable learning experiences for your child's mind and if your child has been wetting the bed at night for many *years*, it won't be surprising if it takes a few *days* to get the problem sorted out.

Imagine taking your car, storing it in a garage and locking it away for 8 or so years. Would you expect to be able to start it first time on taking it out again? Most probably not – you'd need to do a little tweaking and play around with a few wires and maybe even jumpstart it.

It will be a similar experience for getting your child dry at night and all the activities in this book are designed to 'jumpstart' the process of having dry nights forever.

JOSH'S STORY

Josh is aged 9 and his parents brought him along to see me as he was continuing to be wet every night. Having been referred to their local Enuresis Clinic, they had tried pretty much everything. Alarms did not seem to wake him up and when he was prescribed medication, this just made him urinate even more at night-time. He was wearing pull-ups every night and his parents also 'lifted' him just before they went to bed.

They had been trying a variety of methods for over two years with no success. Their doctor suggested they try hypnotherapy as a last resort.

In Josh's school, Year 6 pupils are taken away on a field trip for one week. Josh was beginning to worry – it was becoming more and more important for him to become dry at night, but there did not seem to be a solution.

Josh had two sessions with me – he carried out all the activities and listened to his CD. Rather unusually, Josh was not dry on the first night, nor on the second. By the third night, his parents were ready to abandon things but I persuaded them to stick with it. Josh's habit of night-time wetting was clearly deeply entrenched.

Much to everyone's relief, Josh had a dry night on the fifth night. He continued to have a run of dry nights for over a week before another wet night.

> This turned out to be a 'one-off' and he went on to have another run of dry nights.
>
> Once in a while, he will have a wet night but overall he has managed to completely change his pattern of behaviour from wet to dry.

I've highlighted this particular case for you because it was a bit trickier to solve. But despite struggling to begin with, it wasn't very long after that things just 'clicked' for Josh. 'Sticking with it' proved to be the key to success.

Josh's mum emailed me recently:

"Josh has had a further 6 dry nights in a row and we are all ecstatic. On behalf of all of us, I want to say how grateful we are. Josh seems to be changing too – he seems happier and less moody. It's only now we can see what effect this had on all of us especially Josh – he was becoming so downbeat.

Josh has asked me to say 'I am very happy it has worked and thank you very much'."

HYPNOTIC LANGUAGE

Throughout this book, I've used some well-known hypnotic phrases and sentences – just as I would if you were sitting in a face-to-face session with me. These words are designed to help you see a successful future and feel pumped up and motivated, ready to face your challenge.

It's important to remember that whilst you will have had the benefit of reading these words, your child will not have – unless you decide your child is old enough to read this book and work through the exercises independently, which is possible for teenagers.

So, my advice is to spend plenty of time discussing the ideas in this book with your child before you begin – your child's thought processes will need time to 'catch up' with yours. By all means, repeat some of the words that you've been reading here and get in the habit of using them.

CHAPTER FIVE

•

The Final Countdown

BEFORE YOU BEGIN

To follow this programme there are a few things you will need:

- Sheets of A4 paper

- Felt-tipped pens

- A couple of ordinary party balloons

- Notebook for recording success

- Downloadable audio recording

There's a well-known phrase – "Preparation is 90% of success" and I cannot stress strongly enough how being organised and planning in advance could mean the difference between success and failure for your child. Take the time to think about how you are going to manage the whole business of steering your child towards those dry nights.

PICK YOUR MOMENT

Choosing the right moment to introduce this system to your child is key and it's important to pick your moment carefully. Is your child ready to tackle this problem? Do they recognise that it is something that can be dealt with? Do they have a desire to change?

It's not a good idea to pick a week that you know is going to be a particularly busy one with school exams for example. Likewise if you know you're going to be away from home for a couple of nights or even going away on holiday it may be best to start this programme at a different time.

The school holidays may prove to be the best time for your child, but for others the lack of routine and late nights may cause more problems. You'll know best which week will be right for you – but do plan ahead.

ELECTRICAL EQUIPMENT

I am not a great fan of TVs and computers in children's bedrooms. Nowadays it's easy to become overloaded with electrical gadgets if we include clock radios, mobile phones, TVs, Playstations, computers and Blackberries.

Scientific experts are beginning to agree that sleeping in an electromagnetic field does not aid restful sleep. I would recommend clearing the 'energy space' in your child's bedroom as much as possible by removing as many electrical items as you can.

The visualisation techniques in this book are designed to help your child's brain make new neural connections and wire itself up in a different way. This will be taking place as your child sleeps and dreams – the less interference the better. Playing exciting computer games or watching TV for a short while before going sleep will add to the confusion in your child's mind just at the moment when it will be needed the most. Aim to have a computer/tv-free hour before bedtime.

CLUTTER

Your child is going to be asked to get out of bed and find the route to the bathroom in the middle of the night, should he feel the need to use the toilet. Before doing this, it's worth ensuring that the floor space is completely clear.

Left-over jigsaw puzzles, games, toys and piles of dirty clothes that can be tripped over will not add to your child's confidence about his ability to make it to the bathroom in the dark. A cluttered, disorganised room will reflect your child's cluttered, disorganised mind and this is not going to help him.

Parents can often find getting children to tidy their rooms a bit of a challenge. Be patient with your child and take the time to help them sort things out. Reluctance to tidy a bedroom can seem like 'laziness' but in fact children can often find it difficult to visualise a tidy room and if they can't see it in their imaginations, they won't be able to create it on the outside.

Once your child's room is neat and tidy, it's worth taking a few photographs and leaving them in the room as reference points. In the future you can simply ask your child to make their room look just like it did in the photo.

Avoid using phrases like "Don't leave your room in a mess" for this will only create pictures in their minds of a messy room and it will be very much harder for them to tidy it up. Using sentences like "Let's see if we can get the room nice and tidy" will be very much more helpful to them. Always say what you **do** want to have happen, rather than what you **don't** want.

TOO LIGHT OR TOO DARK?

Some children who come to see me will often reveal in a session that they "would go to the bathroom at night, only it's too dark". Would this apply to your child?

Have a check that the route to the bathroom is well lit. However, whilst it's important to have light on the outside, I would recommend having less light inside the bedroom. Experts do agree that night-lights are best switched off as your child begins to grow up. Your child will experience a deeper, better quality sleep if the room is dark and this alone may ensure a dry night.

If your child really is too scared to visit the bathroom, you could consider placing a potty next to the bed. It may be easier for them just to step out of bed to relieve themselves and once the satisfaction and delight of dry beds has been achieved, you may find their confidence levels boosted enough for the next step. Of course, this does depend entirely on your personal preference and the age of your child. For some children this is a useful 'halfway' measure and it achieves the aim of getting that bed dry.

BATHROOM

And what about the bathroom or toilet? One child who came to see me admitted that he was scared to go to the loo at night because of 'the black toilet seat'. It wasn't so much a case of not wanting to admit it to his mother sooner – it really hadn't occurred to him until he started talking to me about it. It's worth taking the time to make the bathroom as child-friendly as possible.

Position as many items as possible at child-height – eg. mirrors, towel rails, soap and even small wash-hand basins if possible.

Allowing your child to choose some of the accessories, such as colourful hand towels will help your child to feel that this space belongs to him as much as to the adults in the house.

DOUBLE-VOIDING

I've suggested something called 'double-voiding' to a number of children now and it does seem to help. Double-voiding involves going to the toilet *twice* just before going to sleep.

Most children will visit the toilet last thing at night and then spend an extra 20-30 minutes getting ready for bed or reading a story. Others rush in and out of the loo so quickly that they don't fully empty their bladders.

Either way, asking your child to go back into the bathroom a second time before tucking down for the night, ensures that their bladder is completely empty and does seem to help with staying dry all night.

DEEP SLEEPERS

I'm often told by parents that their children are such deep sleepers that they simply do not wake up at night and so it's not possible for them to take themselves to the bathroom at night.

My response to this is 'beware the self-fulfilling prophecy'. Yes – there are some children who are out for the count and nothing will seem to rouse them from a deep, deep sleep – not even lying in a soaking wet bed.

However, it never ceases to amaze me the number of times I have worked with one of these 'deep sleepers' and had them admit in a semi-hypnotic trance that they are in fact aware of wetting their beds – that they do momentarily wake up but they just can't bring themselves to get up and go to the bathroom. Various excuses are then given – they are either slightly afraid (something the parent wasn't aware of, even if steps had been taken to avoid this) or it was simply too cold to contemplate getting out of bed.   After the event, they simply fall back asleep.

I say 'beware the self-fulfilling prophecy' because if this is your child's problem, he or she may well have overheard you repeating this 'deep sleep' mantra many times over either within the family unit or to any of the health professionals that you've consulted in the past.

For years your child could have been hearing that he is a deep sleeper and nothing will wake him up. A nice hypnotic suggestion if ever I heard one!   I wonder how different things could be right now if all your child had heard was what a *light sleeper* they were and how easy it was for them to get up at night and go to the bathroom!

The truth is, we all know that it's very easy to programme our minds to wake up at a specific time. How many times in the past have you had to wake up at some ridiculous hour of the early morning to go on a holiday? Most of us will go to bed worrying about oversleeping only to find ourselves waking up two minutes before the alarm clock goes off. And then we feel strangely spooked by it!

Your child is just as good at programming his or her mind. I bet your child doesn't have problems waking up on Christmas morning or on their birthday. The prospect of receiving those presents is enough to get them jumping out of bed really early in the morning. Without even realising it, they programmed their minds to wake up early, the night before.

And as you'll discover in this programme, it's going to be possible to do the same with waking up to go to the bathroom and avoiding that accident.

FAMILY TREES

I'm often asked if bedwetting runs in families. Many of the parents who come to see me tell me that they were bedwetters until quite late and grandparents can confirm that other members of the family were too.

There's often a desire to trace back through generations and pinpoint the bedwetters in the family and I can understand this as part of your quest to find a reason for your child's problem.

However, I can tell you that I come across far many more bedwetting children *without* a family history than I do children *with*. Perhaps there is a link but for many, there simply isn't.

Again, I worry about the self-fulfilling prophecy here. If your child repeatedly overhears conversations in the family of all the generations before them who had this problem, it's going to be very much harder for them to change. Their self-image (the way that they view themselves) is going be distorted by the evidence that is presented to them of all these bedwetting relatives.

There have been occasions when parents have opened a session with me by saying "I wet the bed until I was ten, so I guess it's going to be the same for my son". And if the child that is over-hearing this is only eight years old, it's very likely that he's not going to fix his problem any time soon.

So, my advice to you is that it doesn't really matter if Auntie Clara, Cousin Jim, Uncle Tom Cobley and all, wet their beds until quite late. It's irrelevant. The only person who is important right now is your child. He or she is a wonderful, unique human being and has the resources and capability to be the master of their own destiny.

CHANGING DRINKING HABITS

There's conflicting advice regarding how many drinks a child who is trying to stop bedwetting, should or shouldn't have each day.

Some experts recommend children drink more water during the day to allow the bladder to stretch and get used to accommodating more liquid at night. Others will recommend restricting drinks and certainly none at all after about 4.30pm in the afternoon.

But then again, some feel that constipation may be one of the reasons for bedwetting – and they would advocate increasing fluids throughout the day.

It's no wonder some parents feel confused.

Personally, I'm not in favour of restricting fluids in young children and certainly not on hot summer days. I feel common sense should prevail – if your child is thirsty, he or she should be able to have a drink.

However, if your child has been advised to drink large quantities of water to stretch their bladder, do ensure that he or she has not got into the habit of gulping and drinking too quickly. Any early evening drinks should be sips of water only and not the huge quantities they may have got used to drinking during the day.

Some of the children who have followed my programme noticed that they were more likely to have a wet bed if they'd had too many sugary, fizzy drinks (including fruit juices) or caffeinated drinks (such as cola, chocolate, tea or coffee) the day before. So, my advice would be 'keep it simple' – let's stick to plain water wherever possible but don't make a big deal of it.

CHANGING EATING HABITS

Did you know that eating certain foods can also have an effect on the bladder – perhaps you've experienced the changes in the smell and colour of your own urine after eating asparagus or beetroot, for example?

Water based fruits and vegetables such as strawberries, melon, grapes, celery and artichokes have a diuretic effect on the body – they encourage you to expel water! I have come across many parents who substitute evening drinks with pieces of fruit so be careful, because you could be causing problems rather than solving them. It's worth doing some research on the internet to see if the foods you are feeding your child have this kind of effect.

It's also known that eating too much wheat can cause a sensitivity in the bladder - whilst the effects are not necessarily noticeable on the outside, the inside of the bladder can become slightly inflamed and as a result hold less urine.

We've become a society that's very dependent on eating a lot of wheat-based products – it's worth thinking about your child's diet and if you find that they eat cereal or toast for breakfast, followed by sandwiches for lunch and then pizza or pasta for dinner, consider making some changes or at least keeping a food diary to see if you can make a connection between the food your child eats and wet nights.

Whilst I'm not in the habit of suggesting exclusion diets, I do think it's worth experimenting for a period of two weeks and cutting out all wheat. Substitute this with more rice or potatoes. Evening meals could consist of jacket potatoes or even chips! Remember, it's just an experiment and is not a regime that your child will follow forever.

It's also been suggested to me by some doctors that milk could be the cause of bedwetting and very often I find that children who come to see me still drink milk at night-time or have had some sensitivity to it in the past.

Another big culprit is the use of artificial sweeteners for they too can have a diuretic effect. These are often hidden in children's food and drinks under the guise of 'healthy' eating, so it's easy not to notice if your child is consuming these. Beware any drinks or fruit squashes that are sugar-free and yoghurts, fromage frais or ice-creams that are low in sugar and labelled 'good for children's teeth' or 'low-calorie'. Go through all your cupboards and read the labels carefully. Eliminate these from your child's diet now.

And rather confusingly, real sugar can also be the cause of wet beds. Most parents would agree that sweet, fizzy drinks will result in a bad night.

Once your child has established a run of dry nights, it won't be surprising if from time to time they have the odd wet night. This will be the perfect time to think back over the previous 24 hours and analyse their food and drink intake to see if you can track down the reason.

Most parents tell me that whenever their children go to a birthday party, they know that they're going to be in for a bad night with several wet beds. It's not surprising given that they've probably consumed just about every known trigger food and drink in the space of a few hours.

One child who came to see me couldn't understand why he'd been dry for several weeks and then during the Christmas holidays had wet his bed several times. "It always happens when I go to Grandma's", he told me. A little further questioning revealed that Grandma loved grapes and each time he visited her, they would sit together in front of the TV eating whole bunches at a time.

If you do find a connection between your child's bedwetting and certain foods, it may be worth consulting a qualified nutritionist who can carry out further tests and help devise suitable menus.

STAYING POSITIVE

It's important to remain encouraging and enthusiastic throughout this period. Remember, the more confident you can appear, the more likely your child is to be successful.

Praise your child regularly and be sympathetic if they have an accident one night. Remind your child that sticking to the exercises will ensure that they have dry nights forever.

For a lot of children, following this programme may mean the situation is going to get worse before it gets better. If your child has been wearing some form of night time protection all his life, this is potentially the first time they will ever have experienced a wet bed. It's not pleasant; it's uncomfortable and it's disruptive.

It's important that you stay strong for your child during this time. Remember, if you do not take the initiative to help solve this problem, your child could be stuck with it for many, many years to come.

We all need a bit of motivation to change the habits in our lives – think back to the last time you wanted to make changes in your life: lose weight, quit smoking or take up exercise for example. You probably thought about doing something for quite a while before you actually got to the point of taking action. Something tipped you over the edge and spurred you into action. It could be the same for your child.

I was contacted by one father who worried because his son had really lost his temper one night – he had kicked his wardrobe door and sobbed 'I'm so fed up with all of this!'.

I reassured the father that this was actually a good sign. And sure enough, one week later I received an email telling me that the boy had been dry every night since.

Think about it – when life is too comfortable there is no incentive for any of us to make changes. – why would we bother? And in just the same way, if your child never experiences a degree of discomfort, his mind will find it much harder to register what 'success' looks and feels like.

No magic fairy is going to fly through your child's bedroom window at night, wave her wand and make your child magically dry at night. It's going to take persistence and training of the right sort. Keeping dry at night is a really important life skill that your child needs to acquire and you are doing absolutely the right thing by putting them on this training path to success.

Too often I have found that parents give in just at the point at which their child was about to turn things around for themselves. Have trust and faith in your child's ability to work through this problem – all you need to do is support them.

Remember, your child is going to encounter many disappointments and failures in his life – we all do.

Your child will not pass every single exam he sits and nor will everyone he meets instantly take a liking to him. Learning how to deal with disappointments by dusting yourself down, picking yourself back up and striving for success once more is going to be one of the very best life lessons your child can learn.

In fact, being a bedwetter could prove to be to your child's *advantage*, rather than *disadvantage* in life. So many times now, I've watched children who've used this system to fix their bedwetting, go on to use the same techniques and approach to achieve success in other areas of their life – be it in the classroom, on the sports field or even on stage.

DEALING WITH ACCIDENTS

It is possible that your child will be dry *every* night from Day 7 of this programme, but it's probably unlikely. Planning in advance will make any accidents much easier to deal with. Have plenty of spare sheets and bedding as well as a plastic protective cover for the mattress.

Consider making up the bed with two layers of sheets and placing an absorbent mat or pad in between these layers. If your child does wet the bed in the middle of the night, you'll be able to quickly remove the top sheet together with the absorbent pad, giving you a ready-made dry bed for him or her to climb into quickly. This will minimise night-time disruptions.

This period of adjustment, should only last a few weeks, so consider organising extra help for yourself if you feel you'll need it. Could wet bedding be sent to the local laundry for example? Could you purchase some extra linen cheaply, to give you plenty of spares to use? The easier you can make life for yourself at this moment, the better support partner you'll be for your child.

Your child is going to need you to stay positive, confident and relaxed with him as you work through this system. Don't let something like a few wet sheets spoil this for you all.

It's a good idea to encourage your child to play a part in changing any wet beds. Some parents groan when they hear this as they have got into the habit of clearing up after their child and worry that getting them involved will be met with resistance but it's an important part of the process of learning how to take responsibility for yourself.

If your child is still quite young, this can be kept to stripping off the wet sheet and putting it in the laundry basket, with an adult finishing things off for them. This is not designed to be a punishment, in the 'you made a mess – you clear it up' vein, but it definitely does help the penny to drop quicker if your child can accept responsibility for the wetness and 'ownership' of the problem. They'll start understanding the consequences of not keeping control of their bladder – as they strip off the bed, that little voice will be chatting away inside their heads, enabling them to think a bit harder about the how, what and why of their problem.

I always tell children that the 'good thing' about problems that we 'own' is that we can find solutions for them much more easily. For example, if a dog walked past your front garden each morning and decided to have a wee against the gate, it's going to be quite hard to get it to change its' behaviour. It's not that easy to change someone or something else. The good thing about your child's bedwetting is that they cause it to happen. And things that you 'start' you can also 'stop'. We can all take control of our own problems.

If asking your child to change sheets every time they're wet seems a bit too much to ask of them, how about picking just two days each week? Negotiate with your child by telling them that you'll be happy to be on 'sheet duty' for five days each week if they take the other two days. Then ask your child to pick which days they think will be the best for them to be on duty eg. weekends or a midweek day when they're not in a rush to get to school.

Having a calendar in the room that reminds them when it's their turn is also a good way of seeing how much they're able to programme their minds to produce a dry night. If your child is always dry when it's his turn to change the sheets, but has a wet night when it's your turn, you'll know you're on to something!

Some children admit to being a bit too lazy to get out of bed to go to the bathroom at night and often asking them to help out with sheet changing is enough to tip the balance. Let's face it, it's easier to nip to the bathroom than change the sheets on a bed!

CONSIDER FINDING A 'BUDDY'

As a mother of three children, I'm all too familiar with the feelings of frustration at being on the receiving end of a child's reluctance to carry out simple tasks, especially if they then willingly perform them for their teachers and tutors. If you feel yourself becoming caught up in a similar situation with this system, then consider using a 'buddy'. This could be a trusted family friend, uncle or aunt, or even a teacher – someone who the child could speak to and liaise with on a regular basis.

Of course, the two of you will still have to be working together with regards to the overall Stop Bedwetting plan, but it may help you to find someone else to carry out the Programme's exercises with them.

CHAPTER SIX

•

The Three Golden Rules

THE THREE GOLDEN RULES

There are just 3 simple rules that I'm going to ask you follow to give your child the best possible chance of success.

RULE NUMBER ONE

No protective pull-up pants or nappies ever again.

Using this system, you'll develop the confidence to clear out the cupboards and rid yourselves of those protective pants that cost a fortune and harm the environment.

By **Day 7** of this programme your task will be to throw them all in the bin. It's important to stick to this rule. Don't be tempted to keep some back 'just in case', as you'll be programming your child's mind for failure rather than success.

However, it is acceptable to use a protective mattress cover in case of accidents. In the meantime, just think how much money you will be saving by never having to buy nappies or protective pants again. Calculate this figure and write it here ....

RULE NUMBER TWO

No lifting.

It's common to receive advice about 'lifting'. This involves waking up your child just as you are going to bed and 'encouraging' them to have one last wee before continuing with the rest of the night's sleep.

On the face of it, sounds like a good idea but not only is it an unpleasant experience for your child (would you like to be woken in the middle of the night and dragged off to the loo?), but you are actively encouraging your child to wee in the night.

It's important to remember what the real goal of this exercise is. Your goal is to help your child achieve night time dryness. By lifting, you are in fact *training* your child to not only release urine when half asleep, but to also develop a need to go to the toilet in the middle of the night. However well intentioned, it's not helpful to the process so let's leave it out.

Do remember to get your child to 'double-void' each night instead.

RULE NUMBER THREE

No Reward Systems

This rule may seem a bit strange as we've become so accustomed to developing reward systems for our children to encourage them to do almost anything. Automatically, we assume that if we want to create a change in behaviour it's not going to be possible without the involvement of star charts, sweeties or trips out.

I'm going to suggest a slightly different approach. It is important to record moments of success and I've provided a special diary for tracking progress further on.

Psychological studies have shown that behaviour that gets measured or observed often improves spontaneously. The attention to detail adds momentum to the process making it easier to achieve our goals.

Combining rewards or treats with a goal-oriented programme however, can just lead to confusion. There's proof that the most helpful way to get your child motivated and successful is to focus on the goal itself – in this case, 'dry beds forever', rather than the 'prize' that will be awarded as a result of it. Remember, your child needs to channel all his brainpower into making that vital connection between the bladder, muscles and the mind – it's best not to create distractions with promises of sweets or trips out to theme parks – you'll actually be making it harder for your child to succeed.

Your child's reward will come naturally, through the possibility of having stress free sleepovers and holidays.

The 3 golden rules are:

1. No pull-ups, nappies or protection at night.

2. No lifting.

3. No reward systems.

This will be your new routine from Day 7 of the programme. In the meantime, if you're still using pull-ups or night-time pants, keep doing so until the instructions tell you to stop.

CHAPTER SEVEN

•

Let's Talk - All About Me

ALL ABOUT ME

Before beginning this programme, there two preliminary activities for you and your child to complete:

Building a positive self-image

Always... Sometimes...... Never

Set aside plenty of time (15 – 20 minutes) to discuss these activities and brainstorm together, perhaps making a few notes first. These activities are designed to put your child into the right frame of mind for making this big change in their lives.

BUILDING A POSITIVE SELF-IMAGE

It's not unusual for children who have a history of wetting their beds at night, to have a poor self-image. This is especially so if the problem has continued for many years.

However hard parents may have tried to minimise the negative impact, it won't have escaped the child's attention that their lives are full of wet, smelly pants or sheets and that they can't quite do what other children can do – such as have sleepovers easily with their friends.

If other methods to solve the bedwetting problem, such as the use of alarms, medication or lifting have also been tried with no success, this will just add to the child's perception of themselves as a failure.

It's really important to reinforce your child's perception of himself as a good, worthwhile, confident and successful person. The more you can build up this image, the more likely your child is to be successful. The pictures we create in our minds with our imaginations play a very big part in determining what happens in our lives.

ACTIVITY 1 - All About me

Step 1:

Complete the details overleaf. Depending on your child's age and writing abilities, this section may be completed by yourself or your child, whichever is easier. Take 15 minutes or so to discuss your child's strengths.

And if your child is of a slightly older age or even a teenager, you can tailor this activity to be more age-appropriate. Change the categories to favourite pop groups, TV programmes, football teams etc. Don't be tempted to skip it out - reassure them that even adults work through a similar self-analysis activity on a coaching programme. The aim of the exercise is to help your child become more self-aware and to boost their confidence before facing the challenge ahead.

Some things about me:

My name is . . . .

My age is . . . .

My favourite colour is . . . .

My favourite food is. . . . .

My friends' names are . . . .

Now make a list of things that your child is good at or found easy to learn – for example: colouring pictures, taking care of a pet, sporting activities, playing musical instruments – these can be as varied and random as you like and as simple or complicated as you'd like.

Things I am good at

. . . .

. . . .

. . . .

. . . .

. . . .

. . . .

. . . .

. . . .

Step 2:

Now ask your child to list activities that they struggled with initially, but eventually mastered –things that were a little trickier to learn, such as riding a bike, swimming, writing their name or learning times tables.

Things I had to practise before I became successful:

. . . .

. . . .

. . . .

. . . .

. . . .

. . . .

. . . .

Remind your child:

Once upon a time, he or she couldn't walk and couldn't talk, or even feed themselves, but gradually over time these were new things that they learnt and can now do quite easily. And the older your child, the longer the list of things that they have mastered in their lives is going to be.

Having dry beds is just one more of those things that they will easily learn.

ACTIVITY 2 – Always, Sometimes, Never

It's interesting how easy it is to get locked into the idea of failure. Once an idea is firmly established in the mind (eg. my child still wets the bed at night), we unconsciously seek out evidence to support this idea. In other words, it will become so easy to remember all those accidents and the wet sheets that needed washing, that we'll cancel out any moments of success.

In this activity, I'm going to ask you to consider the following questions:

*Is your child **always** wet at night?*

*Does he or she **sometimes** have a dry night?*

*Has he or she **never** had a dry night?*

I always ask these questions when parents come to see me with their children. It's very common for them to reply "Well, there was one dry night when we stayed at Grandma's at Christmas...... but that doesn't count.... as we all went to bed so late."

Well – it does count! It very much counts. These odd random moments of dryness are very important...... concrete proof or evidence to your child that they can be dry.... they do have the ability to remain dry throughout the night, they just need a little more practise, that's all.

Fill in the box on the next page and record any successes in relation to dry beds that your child has had in the past. Sometimes a stay at Grandma's or at a friend's house has resulted in a dry night.

If your child has really never had a dry night, is there any other 'evidence' that you can remember that suggests a degree of success – eg. staying dry till 5am in the morning or not being 'lifted' on another occasion. It's important to demonstrate to your child that the same thing doesn't always happen every night. Different things do happen sometimes – they are not locked into a set pattern of behaviour each and every night.

When have I been dry?

. . . .

. . . .

. . . .

. . . .

. . . .

. . . .

. . . .

. . . .

Use this as evidence to demonstrate to your child that they can be successful in achieving this on a permanent basis.

CHAPTER EIGHT

•

My New Future

Day One

MY NEW FUTURE

Welcome to the first day of this life-changing programme for your child. You can spend a few moments reviewing and discussing the preliminary activities from yesterday. Perhaps your child will have thought of a few more ideas to add in to their lists.

There are two activities for you to follow today:

My New Future – Step 1

My New Future – Step 2

MY NEW FUTURE – STEP 1

Today, I'd like you to invite your child to take a glimpse into the future. That wonderful future when everything is just the way he or she would like it to be............... waking up each morning with a dry bed. Begin by asking:

What will you see?

What will you feel?

What will you hear?

Ask your child to draw a picture on the next page showing how fantastic waking up in the morning will be. This is an important step towards getting him or her to be able to visualise a new future clearly. Without this, it will be much harder for them to achieve success.

Include as much information as possible – the bed with dry sheets, the time on the clock and perhaps even the weather outside.

Ask your child to remember to include themselves in the picture .... with a big smile on his or her face. They can add in other people, perhaps having them speaking some words. Encourage your child to write a sentence at the bottom of the picture along the lines of:....

It is .... (fill in the important date you've chosen to be dry by) and I'm waking up with a dry bed. I see my nice, clean dry sheets and the smile on my mother's face. I feel happy and confident and I hear myself whoop with delight.

You can play around with the details in this sentence to suit.

Note: if your child is really reluctant to draw pictures, you can ask them to describe the scene in detail to you and make notes instead. The aim of the exercise is to get as much detail as possible recorded – remember to answer the questions at the beginning of the exercise.

MY NEW FUTURE LOOKS LIKE THIS:

Complete this sentence: When I have dry beds in the morning, this is what I will see, hear and feel:

....

....

....

MY NEW FUTURE – STEP 2

Now take a few moments to encourage your child to think about what else will happen as a result of having dry beds. Ask the following questions:

As well as having a dry bed, what else will change in your life? Will it change the way you feel?

And what about the other people around you? How will they feel? Imagine who else will be there first thing in the morning and the kind of things that they might say.

Imagine yourself being successful and having dry beds - will it mean you can start to do different things, like have sleepovers with friends? Will it mean you can go on holidays and school trips more easily?

What's the very best thing that will happen to you when you are dry at night?

What will you see?

What will you hear?

What will you feel?

Complete this sentence: When I have dry beds it will mean

that ....

....

Ask your child to pick two examples and draw pictures below to show how much better things will look.

CHAPTER NINE

•

Mind over body

Day Two

MIND OVER BODY

Welcome to Day 2 of the programme – progress is being made.

As before, take a few moments to discuss and review the ideas that came up for you and your child in the previous activities. Talking will help reinforce ideas in your child's mind.

There are **two** new activities for you to cover today:

How My Body Works

Controlling Muscles

HOW MY BODY WORKS

It's important for your child to have a better understanding of how the body works and what it's going to be asked to do. Explain to your child that the mind and body are connected and have a conversation with each other throughout the day.

Sometimes our bodies tell us what to do and sometimes we tell our bodies what to do.

Your body tells you:

- If you're too hot - *you might want to take your jumper off*

- If you're too cold - *you'll feel like putting a jumper on*

- If you're hungry - *your tummy will start to rumble*

- If you're thirsty - *your mouth will feel dry*

- If you're tired - *you'll start yawning*

And then there are those other times when you tell your body to do things:

- You tell it to run
- You tell it to jump
- You tell it to speak out loud
- You tell it to pick up a pencil and write

And telling your body to *hang on and walk* to the bathroom to use the toilet if you need to, is just one more of those things you'll be able to teach it to do.

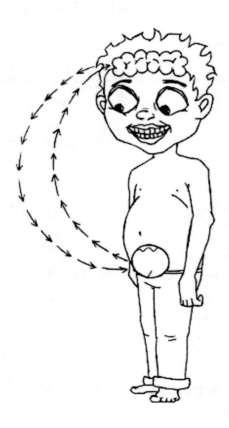

CONTROLLING MUSCLES

The bladder is a pouch or bag made of muscle that opens and closes as it tenses and relaxes.

Our bodies are full of muscles that can do this – we have them in our arms and legs, fingers and toes and we can tell them exactly what to do. We tell the muscles in our bodies to do things all the time.

Take a few moments, find a quiet space to sit or lie down with your child and discover what I mean as you play this game with your child.

Hands: *Clench each fist (one at a time) for three seconds and then relax it for three seconds.*

Arms: *Bend each elbow so the wrist nearly touches the shoulder (one at a time) and hold for 3 seconds, then relax each arm for 3 seconds.*

Legs: *Point the toes and straighten the leg, pushing the knee down, so both the calf and thigh muscles tighten for 3 seconds, then relax this leg for 3 seconds. Repeat with the other leg.*

Shoulders: *Pull the shoulders up to the ears (or as close as they can get) and hold for 3 seconds, then relax for a further 3 seconds.*

Eyes: *Scrunch up the eyes so that they are tightly shut for 3 seconds. Then relax the eyes, but keep them shut for at least 3 seconds.*

CHAPTER TEN

•

Close that Gate

Day Three

CLOSE THAT GATE

Yesterday, you discovered how your mind and body work by talking to each other. And you also discovered how you can make those muscles tighten and then relax again, simply by thinking about it.

In just the same way, it's possible to control the bladder – opening it and closing it as and when needed. The muscles act like a 'gate' on the bladder.

Try this experiment and you'll see what I mean.

Handy tip: trying this in the bath may be the best place!!

WATER BALLOON EXPERIMENT

1. Take an ordinary party balloon (a round one is best) and attach it to the end of a cold water tap.

2. Switch the tap on slowly and watch as the water begins to fill the balloon. Keep going until it's a bit bigger than a tennis ball. Switch the water off.

Now, very carefully take the balloon off the tap and squeeze the open end between your thumb and one of your fingers, to make sure the water can't come out.

3. Turn the balloon upside down over the sink. This is similar to how your bladder looks. Slowly, begin to relax your fingers slightly and allow some water to begin trickling out of the end. This is just how water comes out of your bladder when you go to the toilet.

4. Now let's see if we can stop this flow. Squeeze your fingers tight once more and you'll discover that you can easily stop the water coming out.

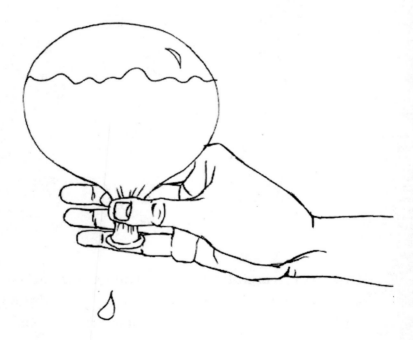

6. And then squeeze them tightly shut to stop the flow once more.

This is exactly how your muscles work – squeezing tight to hold urine in the bladder and relaxing to let it out – just like opening and closing a gate.

You can practise this exercise again, if you want to. Keeping this gate tightly closed is just what your body needs to learn to do at night to help you keep your bed dry.

DRINKING EXERCISE

You can follow this exercise with some drinking practice. Ask your child to drink a large glass of water and wait for it to fill up their bladder. Then when they need to, they can go to the toilet and practise using those muscles by stopping and starting the flow of urine.

Suggest to them that they can practise stopping and starting their wee like this, several times a day – opening and closing their gate.

GATE VISUALISATION

Now that we know how the muscles in our body open and close around the bladder just like a gate, we're going to take a closer look at your child's 'gate'. Everyone's is different and I wonder what his or hers will look like.

---

1. *Settle yourselves down somewhere comfortable. Ask your child to close his eyes and just take a few moments to visualise the gate to his bladder. Pause for a few moments to give your child time to do this.*

2. *Encourage him to describe it clearly to you*

    - *what colour is it?*
    - *how does it open?*
    - *does it have a lock or bolt on it?*
    - *is the lock tightly shut right now?*

3. *Ask your child to tell you what needs to be done to make sure this gate is firmly shut at night. (Allow your child's imagination to take over here – some children invent gatekeepers, or put extra big locks on- others even have pets or animals keeping guard.)*

Ensure your child's gate will not leak – many children visualise a gate that's similar to their own garden gate and this may not be suitable for holding back a liquid. Use the word 'door' if you feel this would be more appropriate..

Now ask your child to draw a picture of this gate here.............

My gate looks like this!!

CHAPTER ELEVEN

•

Pump up the volume!

Day Four

PUMP UP THE VOLUME

Welcome to Day 4 – you're halfway through the programme now.

Take some time to review and chat about the exercises from the previous days. If you feel there is any confusion or lack of understanding, you'll be able to remind your child that each day they are getting closer and closer to achieving their goal – Dry Nights Forever!

There are two more exercises to carry out today:

Volume Control Exercise

Saying What you Want

Note: from tomorrow your child will need to start listening to the Hypnotic Recording – Dry Beds Now. If you haven't done so already, DOWNLOAD it from my website now – www.stopbedwettingin7days.co.uk . – it's free of charge and getting it now will mean that you'll have it to hand when you need it.

VOLUME CONTROL EXERCISE

Some nights it isn't going to be possible to wait until morning to visit the toilet - some nights your child may need to get up and go to the loo. We already know this.

But in the past, your child's mind and body just haven't been communicating well enough to enable this to happen. Your child has remained in bed and you've dealt with the consequences in the morning.

During the day, your child gets messages from the bladder many times. A little voice gets heard in the mind – *"need to go to the toilet"* – and your child responds by walking to the bathroom and successfully dealing with the situation. Point this out to your child and ask them to pay specific attention to what receiving this message feels like, for the next few days.

During the night your child is asleep. So when that little voice pipes up – *"need to go to the toilet"* – it doesn't get heard.

There's a very simple solution to this. Let's turn the volume UP!!!

Take a few moments to run through this activity with your child. Begin by explaining to your child that he hears that little voice inside his head many times a day. It not only speaks up when it needs to go to the loo, but it's the same voice that says

"hmm, I'm hungry, I fancy a biscuit"

"I'm feeling hot – I want to take my jumper off"

"I wonder what's on television"

and getting it to speak a little louder at night time, is just one of those things that can easily be done.

1. *Ask your child to think of a favourite piece of music. This could be a song that they really like, the theme tune to a TV programme or even the 'Happy Birthday' song.*

2. *Ask them to tell you what it is and to just let themselves hear that music playing in their imaginations – ie. not out loud. Keep playing this music for a few moments.*

3. *Now it's time for a bit of fun. Get your child to play around with the volume by saying "I wonder if you can make it just a little bit quieter? And a little bit quieter still?" Pause here for a few moments to allow your child to do this.*

4. *And now you can turn the volume up by saying "And how about making it louder? .... And a bit more?......... I wonder if you can make it so loud that it would wake the baby/frighten the dog (or similar)". Again pause for a few moments to allow your child to do this. It's usual to see an intense look of concentration accompanied by a few giggles as they get the hang of this.*

5. *Take a few more moments to play around turning the volume back down so it's nice and quiet and up, up, up so it's really loud once more.*

THE VOLUME CONTROL

We don't know what your child's volume control looks like. Each one of us has a control that looks slightly different.

Point out to your child some of the different controls that can be found around the house – for example: the light switch that flicks on and off, or maybe it's a dimmer that rotates around. Some switches are dials, others are levers and some have buttons like the controls for the television.

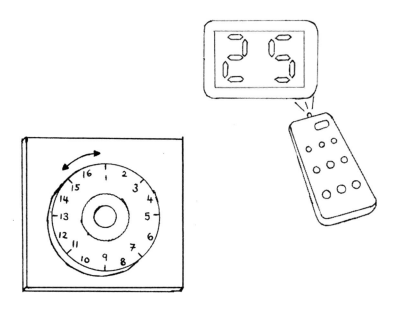

1. Ask your child to close his eyes for a few moments to take a really good look at the volume control that controls the sounds inside his mind.

2. What colour is it? How about the shape – is it round, square or long? Does it have a dial or a button?

3. How does he know which setting it's on – does it have numbers 1-10 or higher? Or does it say Low-Medium-High?

4. Ask your child to play around with the volume setting – can they turn it right down low? And then right up high, so it's very much louder?

Ask your child to draw a picture of his very own special volume control here:

This is my volume control!

Now that we know what that all important volume control looks like, your child will be able to easily programme it each night before going to sleep.

AUTOMATIC PILOT

We've all had situations where we've had to get up extra specially early in the morning – perhaps to go off on holiday and catch an early morning flight.

Have you ever set the alarm clock for some crazy time like 4am, worried that you might oversleep but somehow miraculously found yourself automatically waking up five minutes before the alarm goes off?

It's a strange feeling, isn't it? People often wonder why that happens - in reality, not only do we set the alarm clock but we also programme our subconscious minds to wake us up as we're doing it. So, when we wake up early, we're literally operating on 'automatic pilot'.

In just the same way, your child can programme his very own 'automatic pilot' to wake himself up when he receives that signal from his bladder.

ADJUSTING THE VOLUME

1. *Ask your child to close his eyes and see in his imagination the volume control for the bladder – this may look a little different to the one that was controlling the music – check with your child and ask him to describe it once more.*

2. *What is the control set at? Is it set on high? Or is it set on low? Should it be adjusted?*

3. *Pause for a few moments here to allow your child to make whatever adjustments he or she feels are necessary to set this volume control on a loud enough setting to wake him up during the night, should he need to visit the toilet.*

Every evening just before settling down for the night, your child will need to run through this activity and just check the control is set at the right level.

WHAT YOU <u>SAY</u> IS WHAT YOU <u>SEE</u>

As we've already discovered, our minds are constantly making pictures in response to the words that come into our minds. If I ask you now NOT to think of a piece of chocolate cake, there'll be no prizes for guessing what picture comes straight into your mind. Whether you wanted to or not, chocolate cake is what you saw.

Your mind had no option but to do this, as there's no picture it can make for the word *'not'* – so you got left with precisely what you didn't want to see.

That's why it's going to be really important to be conscious of the words that you speak to your child whilst working through this programme. The emphasis is going to be on having 'dry beds' rather than 'not having wet beds'.

We are magnetically drawn towards the pictures we make in our imaginations – so it's important to always be making good ones.

SAYING WHAT YOU WANT

Keeping in mind the importance of thinking and saying what it is we DO want to happen, rather than what we DON'T want to happen, ask your child to spend a few moments each evening saying the following phrases out loud just before going to bed each night.

These phrases will be the equivalent of setting that alarm clock – your child's automatic pilot:

"While I'm sleeping tonight bladder, if you start filling up – be sure to send a really loud message to my brain to let me know".

"Turn the volume up really loud, so that I can hear you".

"And remember to keep the gate shut until you wake me up, so I can get up out of my dry bed and walk to the bathroom in time."

Saying these phrases slowly, deliberately and out loud will send a flow of energy, almost like a crackle of electricity, down a particular neural pathway creating that vital link between mind and body.

Handy Tip : Either you or your child can copy these sentences out onto sticky post-it notes and stick them on the wall next to the bed. Each evening, just before tucking down to sleep, your child will be able to say them out loud once more.

CHAPTER TWELVE

•

Programming your Sat-Nav

Day Five

PROGRAMMING YOUR SAT-NAV

Welcome to Day 5. Praise your child for having done really well to get this far. There are not too many days to go now. Remind him that in just a couple of days, he'll be enjoying the benefits of having those 'dry nights'.

As your programme progresses and the activities begin to build up, you may want to review yesterday's at a different time to introducing the new ones today. There is just one visualisation exercise to carry out today and your child will need to start listening to the Hypnotic Recording – "Dry Beds Now!!" – which you can get free from my website at *www.stopbedwettingin7days.co.uk*.

Have you downloaded your copy yet?

Today's activities are:

Sat Nav Programming

Listening to Hypnotic Recording

SAT- NAV PROGRAMMING

Most of us wouldn't set off on a long journey without putting our destination into our satellite navigation systems, printing off directions from the internet or checking a map. Only when we have a pretty good idea of where we're heading and how to get there, do we set off.

Expecting your child to get up in the middle of the night, in the dark and visit the bathroom in a semi-conscious state is a bit like playing 'Blind-man's Buff' at a children's party. It's no wonder most kids opt to stay in bed and not venture out. So how can we give your child a map to navigate by?

Step One

Begin by starting this activity during the daytime when there is some light and it is a little less daunting. After the first couple of attempts, you can close the bedroom curtains to make it more realistic. It's really important to reinforce your child's perception of himself as someone who can easily get up and walk to the bathroom at night, should they need to. The more this is 'rehearsed', the more likely your child is to be successful.

1. *Ask your child to climb into bed and snuggle down under the covers, as if going to sleep at night.*

2. *Next, ask him/her to imagine that they've just received the signal that it's time to go to the loo. Ask them to turn the volume up and really hear that voice inside their head.*

3. *Guide your child out of bed and walk slowly together along the route to the bathroom.*

4. *As you're walking along describe the route out loud: eg. turn left, straight along for six steps, out of the door, into the hallway, eight steps past the cupboard and Mum and Dad's bedroom, a few more steps and into the bathroom. Describe the route exactly as you see it.*

5. *Repeat this process several more times, until your child knows it off by heart and can say it out loud by themselves.*

Step Two

Having established the best route for your child to use at night time, it's time to ensure that this becomes firmly imprinted on your child's mind by rehearsing it over and over again. This way, their personal "sat-nav" system is fully programmed.

Remember, if your child needs to go to the loo during the night, he or she will only be semi-conscious – this needs to be something they can do without thinking.

1. *Ask your child to lay down on the bed once more and close their eyes. Once again, ask them to imagine that they've just received the signal (ie. heard that very loud voice) from their bladder that they need to go to the loo.*

2. *This time, they can allow themselves to just picture themselves walking to the bathroom in their imagination. They won't need to do it 'for real', but your child will need to describe the route to the bathroom out loud a couple of times over. As you listen to this, check that their details are correct.*

3. *Now they'll be ready to just run through the scenario in their minds without saying anything at all. Repeat this several times over.*

Remember – our bodies can't tell the difference between a real and an imagined event. This is a very clever way of 'rehearsing' the future, tricking your body into believing that you have done this before - making it all the easier to do it 'for real' when the time comes.

LISTENING TO THE AUDIO RECORDING

Have you downloaded your FREE audio recording from my website yet?

www.stopbedwettingin7days.co.uk

This audio recording called 'Dry Beds Now' lasts around twenty minutes. Your child will need to have a quiet place to listen to this. It's filled with positive messages which will reinforce all the work we've done so far.

It can be listened to once your child is in bed, in place of a bedtime story. However, as it's possible they will drift off to sleep whilst listening to it, I'd recommend giving them the opportunity to listen to it earlier in the day too. It's not necessary to be lying down with eyes closed – if your child is having a quiet moment playing with puzzles for example, you can have the recording playing in the background.

Please DO NOT play it whilst you are driving in the car or operating machinery. It's very relaxing!!

NOTE: If your child finds this audio recording a little 'young' for them, it is possible to purchase a different one from my website. 'Stop Bedwetting Now' is designed for children and teenagers.

Before your child goes to sleep tonight, I recommend running through this short list of activities.

TONIGHT'S BEDTIME CHECKLIST

- Visualise gate on bladder and close it tight. ☐

- Set volume control on HIGH. ☐

- Speak 'auto-pilot phrases' out loud. ☐

- Programme Sat Nav ☐

- Listen to audio recording. ☐

CHAPTER THIRTEEN

•

Booking a Wake Up Call

Day Six

BOOKING A WAKE UP CALL

Welcome to Day Six of this programme. In Chapter Five I talked about how 'self-image' can play a part in our ability to overcome problems and change habits. Many parents tell me that their child is a deep sleeper and nothing will wake them up – not even a traditional bedwetting alarm. Often this disturbs the entire household and not the child it was intended for.

I believe that rather than relying on an alarm on the 'outside' to wake your child, it would be better if he or she built one on the 'inside'.

Over time, your child will have gathered much evidence to support the notion that "nothing will wake him" either through over-hearing this being said about him or through direct experience.

Step 1

It's time to gather evidence to the contrary. Your child has the ability to wake himself up at a particular time very easily. Think back to some of these occasions:

- Christmas or traditional festival

- Birthday

- First day back at school

- Holiday

- Arrival of a new sibling or family pet

- Return of a parent from a business trip

- School play

- Exams

- First date

I'm sure you can think of many more. A mixture of excitement and anxiety the night before an event meant your child 'programmed' his mind to wake up at a particular time and most likely, woke up five minutes before he was due to. We've all done this and most of us wondered how it happened.

Let's do some programming right now:

Just as you did in the earlier exercise 'Always, Sometimes, Never', I'd like you sit down with your child and ask him to remember all those occasions when he did wake up extra early.   Write them down, make a list and discuss this for around 15 minutes.

Point out how everything that they did the night before be it:

- packing a suitcase

- hanging up Christmas stockings

- last minute revision

- laying out special clothes

all contributed to the 'programming' part of the wake-up process.   Not only were they performing these tasks but also making very clear pictures inside their minds of the forthcoming events.   They then went to sleep with these pictures milling around inside their heads and, lo and behold, they woke up early.

Step 2

In the second part of today's activities, you're going to ask your child to build an alarm for themselves. To trigger off your child's creative processes, I often refer to action movies such as 'James Bond'.   Quite often the final 15 minutes of this type of film involves a timer, clock or buzzer counting down two minutes before some kind of explosion or eruption occurs. This may inspire your child.

On the other hand, I've come across many children for whom the word 'alarm' can be quite upsetting – especially if they've used a bedwetting alarm in the past. And of course, alarms are often associated with emergency situations so it's not surprising. Choose your terminology carefully and ensure it suits your child.

They could choose a buzzer, a bell or even use music. Perhaps they would prefer a 'buddy' to stand by the gate to their bladder and keep a watchful eye – as soon as their bladder reaches 98% full, it could be the Buddy's job to sound the signal.

1. *Pick a quiet moment and ask your child to lay down on his or her bed and take a few moments to relax. They can do this exercise with their eyes open or closed – whichever suits them best.*

2. *Ask them to visualise the gate on their bladder once more – perhaps this is an ideal opportunity to make any adjustments or changes to it. Does it look as if it will leak? Should it be altered in any way?*

170 | S T O P   B E D W E T T I N G   I N   7   D A Y S

3. *Once this has been done, explain that it's time to put in an extra 'early warning system'. Ask your child to be creative here and design a system that feels right for them.*

4. *Some children choose to put glass panels on the side of their bladders so the buddy can see how quickly it's filling up. Others will create a sensor that can in some way detect this. And then it's important to create a button, lever or dial that will trigger off the sound.*

5. *Allow your child to experiment with sounds. Remember that volume control from the earlier exercise. Does your child wish to create speakers either side of the gate to really boom out the sound of the wake up call.*

6. *And when does your child want the wake up call to go off? When his bladder is full might just be too late. Would he prefer to set it for a couple of minutes beforehand to enable him plenty of time to get out of bed and off to the bathroom. All these details need organising.*

When your child is finished, offer him a large sheet of paper and some coloured pens. Ask him to draw the picture that he saw.

Some children create quite complicated alarm systems that can tie them up in knots. Whilst it's important for children to create this for themselves, I do feel it is fine to guide them a little to get a clear picture in their minds of how the whole system will work.

TONIGHT'S BEDTIME CHECKLIST

- Visualise gate on bladder and close it tight. ☐

- Set volume control on HIGH. ☐

- Speak 'auto-pilot phrases' out loud. ☐

- Programme Sat Nav ☐

- Check your Wake Up Call is set ☐

- Listen to audio recording. ☐

CHAPTER FOURTEEN

•

Overcoming Doubts

Day Seven

OVERCOMING LAST MINUTE DOUBTS

As you and your child reach the final day of preparation for your new life of "DRY BEDS FOREVER", now is the time to take a few moments to just check if there are any last minute doubts, worries or niggles that could hold your child back. Tonight, you'll be repeating several of the activities.

Tomorrow you'll be leaving those protective pull-up pants or nappies behind forever. The time for collecting up every last one in the house and disposing of them for good is not very far away.

First of all, it's important to check that each and every 'part' of you and your child is happy with the decision to move forward in this way. It's common to feel in 'two minds' about certain things because two minds is exactly what we have – our conscious mind and our subconscious mind. It's easy to feel as if we know what we want to achieve on the outside but sometimes, our insides can almost 'sabotage' our attempts.

How many of us adults want to lose weight but on the other hand, also really fancy that extra piece of chocolate cake? Have you ever wanted to get fit and go to the gym, but on the other hand really wanted to stay on the sofa and watch a movie?

The same goes for our children. Perhaps on the one hand they really want to spend time doing their school homework to get good marks, but on the other hand they also want to spend time playing a video game or watching TV.

Success becomes much harder to achieve when there's a little bit of an internal struggle going on. Take a few moments now to discuss any last doubts or worries that both of you may be having.

Perhaps you're really looking forward to having dry nights forever with no more pull-ups, but on the other hand you also want to ensure the bed sheets are dry. On the one hand, it would be nice to save lots of money from not having to buy protective pants or pull-ups but, on the other hand, will the money be spent on lots of extra washing of wet sheets?

Perhaps your child is looking forward to having sleepovers with their friends, but, on the other hand, the safety and security of home where they can keep their pull-ups on is also appealing?

All of these negative feelings are serving a purpose – they are trying to protect you and your child and their intention is good. Even though it feels as if you are being pulled in two different directions, both sides only want the best for you. However, those feelings can have a sabotaging effect and hold you back from what you'd really like to achieve. Always keep in mind your ultimate goal – what would you really like to have happen? What is your dream?

ACHIEVING AGREEMENT

1. Take a few moments to identify any last minute worrying beliefs that you or your child may have. You may want to discuss these issues and write them down on a piece of paper.

2. Once you have done this, place your hands out in front of you with your palms facing up to the ceiling. Imagine the part that wants dry beds in your right hand and the other part, the bit that sometimes holds you back, in your left.

3. As you look at each hand in turn, ask the part what its' positive intention is for you. Continue asking each part until it becomes increasingly obvious that they both want the same thing for you – namely, dry beds, success and happiness.

4. Keep running through this process, even if it feels a little strange to begin with. Doing this will create changes in your confidence and self-belief.

5. Imagine a new 'super-part' emerging in the space between your hands. A 'super-part' that has the resources to keep both of those other parts happy and still create success for you. As you look down into this space, you may want to give it a colour – a special colour - a colour that feels right for you.

6. *Now moving quickly, bring your hands together and allow those two separate parts to merge with the super-part and become one.*

7. *Raise your hands up to your chest and bring them in, allowing this new 'super' part to become fully absorbed and integrated as a new bit of you.*

8. Close your eyes and enjoy this feeling of having every bit of your body in agreement about the kind of future you'll have.

As you practise this technique, you'll find all those feelings of internal conflict begin to simply disappear. You and your child both have a goal in mind – dry beds forever – and as all those parts line up in agreement, you'll find it easier to achieve just that.

TONIGHT'S BEDTIME CHECKLIST

- Visualise gate on bladder and close it tight. ☐

- Set volume control on HIGH. ☐

- Speak 'auto-pilot phrases' out loud. ☐

- Programme Sat Nav ☐

- Check your Wake Up Call is set ☐

- Listen to audio recording. ☐

CHAPTER FIFTEEN

●

Day Eight and Beyond

DRY NIGHTS FOREVER

Well done – you've reached the end of the programme and the beginning of that new future.

Each day for the next week, it's going to be important for your child to continue to listen to the Hypnotic Recording that you've downloaded.

Additionally, there'll be that bedtime checklist of activities to run through.

NO MORE PROTECTIVE NIGHT-TIME PANTS

You have now reached the moment where you can throw out those nappies, pull-ups, alarms – whatever it is you were using at night, but remember it's still OK to protect the bed using absorbent mats or sheets.

Spend some time with your child and hunt through your cupboards, under the beds and even in the garage, to track down every last pull-up in the house. Bundle them all together in a plastic sack and throw them as far away as possible – certainly not in the house!! As your child's mind and body start to work closer together now than ever before, you'll both discover that you no longer have a need for them.

Really enjoy this moment together - this is an important step forward in your child's development and the more confident you can be as you do this, the more confident your child will feel.

I am often asked by clients "Should I keep a couple of pull-ups just in case?". As tempting as this will be, I would recommend that you do not do this. "Just in case" or "for emergencies" really means "in case this doesn't work" and you'll be programming your mind to do just that – fail. Programme your mind for success and you'll succeed.

More importantly, getting rid of the pull-ups is sending a clear message to your child that you really expect them to succeed. Remember, we transmit messages through our body language and our actions as well as our words.

BEDTIME CHECKLIST

- Repeat clenching muscles and balloon exercises as often as you like.   ☐

- Visualise gate on bladder and close it tight.   ☐

- Set volume control on HIGH.   ☐

- Speak 'auto-pilot phrases' out loud.   ☐

- Programme Sat Nav   ☐

- Check your Wake Up Call is set   ☐

- Listen to audio recording   ☐

RECORDING SUCCESS

Keeping track of progress will spur your child on to even greater success. Tell your child that from now on he is going to have to behave a little like a 'detective' – noticing small changes, collecting evidence and proof that he is moving closer and closer each day to his goal.

It's going to be important to keep a record of all successes, big and small, rather than simply keeping a record of dry nights or wet nights. There may be the occasional wet night and, if this does happen, your child's 'detective' powers will need to be even more special.

Record any proof or evidence of successfully keeping to the system and leaving old habits and behaviours behind. This could be as simple as listening to the recording before bedtime and carrying out some of the visualisation exercises. Even the act of going to bed without wearing protective pants is a huge step forward and deserves to be recorded as success. So, even if an accident occurs, there is still 'progress' that can be captured.

Some children report that, on occasions, although they didn't quite make it to the bathroom in time, they did wake up in time to be aware of wetting the bed. If in the past, your child would normally have slept right the way through, then they have made 'progress'. It demonstrates that the messages are getting through, the system is working and they'll most probably be dry the next night.

Let's not forget, each small step forward, however small, is one step further forward in the process of having dry nights forever. The more 'success steps' you can record, the more you'll be helping your child to reach their overall goal.

You can either record your child's progress in the spaces provided below or you can buy a separate notebook or diary for your child to use. As well as making a note of events on a daily basis, your child can also use this book to remind themselves of how different life will be in the future.

Encourage your child to be creative – maybe drawing more pictures or sticking in photos of friends he'd like to have sleepovers with, or even pictures of places he may go to on overnight school trips.

Remember, all the children who have used this system with me have been really successful, really quickly.

MY SUCCESS RECORD

These were my successes today:

Date : . . . .

. . . .

. . . .

Date : . . . .

. . . .

. . . .

Date : . . . .

. . ..

. . . .

Date : . . . .

.. . .

.. . .

MY SUCCESS RECORD

These were my successes today:

Date : . . . .

. . . .

. . . .

Date : . . . .

. . . .

. . . .

Date : . . . .

. . . .

. . . .

Date : . . . .

. . . .

. . . .

<u>MY SUCCESS RECORD</u>

These were my successes today:

Date : . . . .

. . . .

. . . .

Date : . . . .

. . . .

. . . .

Date : . . . .

. . . .

. . . .

Date : . . . .

. . . .

. . . .

COOLING OFF PERIOD

Once your child has been achieving dry nights for a few weeks, you can begin winding the activities down. I suggest that the hypnotic recording is listened to just once or twice a week.

You can also review some of the exercises a couple of times during the week. It's very likely that your child will have got into a routine and will automatically repeat most of the exercises, without needing a reminder.

If your child continues to be dry, you'll be able to reduce to just once a week and see how things go.

CELEBRATING SUCCESS

Having successfully worked your way through this programme, you and your child will be able to look forward to that new future with 'dry beds forever'.

This is not magic, but you might be surprised to discover that it might *seem* like magic ....

Enjoy those sleepovers!

Alicia

CHAPTER SIXTEEN

•

Frequently Asked Questions

FREQUENTLY ASKED QUESTIONS

Here are some of the most common questions I get asked by parents who ask me to help their children with their bedwetting problems.

Q. At what age do children usually become dry at night?

A. There's a complex co-ordination that needs to develop between nerves and muscles in order to control the bladder. This has usually taken place by the age of 5 but some children take a little longer. If your child has reached his or her 6th birthday and still regularly wets the bed, it's a good idea to consider this system to help them become dry.

Q. How old does my child have to be to use this system?

A. Your child will need to be old enough to understand the problem and how they have a part to play in getting themselves dry and this will vary from child to child. All the techniques described in this book are suitable for use with young children and I have worked in similar ways with children as young as four years.

Q. My child is not only wet at night but also has accidents during the day. He gets distracted and leaves it too late to visit the toilet resulting in wet patches on his trousers. Can this system help?

A. Whilst this programme is not specifically designed to help with day time accidents, many parents do find that working through the exercises does help to build up the child's self-awareness and as a result day time wetness becomes a thing of the past. Many children fix their day time habits before their night time ones, so applaud their progress and point it out to them, even if they haven't achieved dry nights yet. They are on the right track.

Q. What happens if we miss doing the activities on one of the days?

A. Continue to work through the system on the next available day. Ensure your child can remember the previous activities well enough before moving on to the next one. Don't attempt to 'catch up' by doing two day's activities in one and remember to alter any dates you may have marked in the calendar. However, once your child starts to listen to the CD, it's best not to miss a day for at least one week.

Q. I can't eliminate all pull-up pants from the house as my child's 3 year old sister is still wearing them at night. Is this a problem?

A. It's worth finding a new place to store younger siblings' protective night pants, perhaps even providing a new box or container for them to clearly indicate who they belong to. If they share a bedroom do store them as far away as possible.

Q. My child has been dry for 6 nights but wet on the 7th. It was the same story the following week – dry for 6 nights but wet again on the 7th. Should I be thinking about doing something differently?

A. No – your child has had 12 dry nights out of 14. That's fantastic progress – you've clearly being doing everything right and there's no need to think about changing anything. Remember to focus on your child's successes rather than any accidents that may occur along the way.

Q. I can't seem to get my child to follow one of the visualisation exercises – is this going to be a problem?

A. The more exercises your child can take part in, the better – however, it's not essential to follow each one in order to have this process work. It's important for your child to have an understanding of how the mind and body work closely together and it's also important for your child to listen to the CD for several days.   Thereafter, there is a degree of flexibility in the system. Whilst I believe it's best to work through all the activities, I have had children who have become completely dry by just listening to my CD and doing no more.

Q. Is listening to the audio recording an essential part of this programme? I feel my child is getting fed up of listening to it.

A. Different things work for different children and not everyone will get along with a listening activity and may prefer to do some drawing or writing instead. However, personally I would recommend it. Could you make it easier for your child by playing it in the background as they do other activities such as play with a puzzle on the floor? Would listening to it through a headset, whilst travelling to school in the car be a more appealing way of doing it?

Two other CDs are available from my website – Stop Bedwetting Now, which is designed for children up to teenage years and A Magic Day Out which is a general confidence boosting, habit-busting story for 5-12 year olds.

Q.My child has had some success but now seems to be getting despondent and angry what can I do?

A.Hang on in there and don't be tempted to go back to old habits of wearing night time protection pants or lifting. It's important to keep moving forwards and remembering that this is a really important life skill that your child needs to acquire. Following this programme means you're making life better for him, not worse – it may just take a bit of time for him to realise that too.

Q.My child has been dry for several months now but each time we visit the grandparents, he wets the bed. It's so embarrassing – how can I get him to stop? I know he's happy with the visits and I've checked his bedroom is cosy and he's not scared by anything there. What do you suggest?

A. This may not be purely coincidental and I would recommend taking a close look at what your child has to eat and drink whilst staying there. It could be triggered off by sugar-free squashes, fizzy drinks, drinking milk, eating too much fruit or wheat. It's worth writing everything down and this should give you some clues as to why this could be happening.

Q.My son has been really successful – 6 dry nights in a row. But now he's had 3 wet nights and is getting disheartened. How can I explain to him that this is normal?

It's a good idea to remind him that this is not the first time in his life that he's had to practise something before getting good at it (give him examples).

When children first learn how to swim, the teacher tells them what to do and how to move their arms and legs. To begin with, they have to "think" about what they're doing and concentrate quite hard. This is the conscious mind working.

And then, as time goes by they get the hang of it and before they know it they can swim and chat to their friends at the same time. Their behaviour is now imprinted on their subconscious minds. And how good does that feel?

So, things are going well and then one day they go swimming and for some reason, it's a struggle. Things just don't go as well as they usually do – it's an "off" day. Those are the sort of days when mums and dads will be saying "I don't know what his problem is...... last week he could do backstroke perfectly and now he's all over the place!" Does this sound familiar?

It's the same for any kind of new behaviour that our bodies are trying to learn – sometimes we have 'off' days. But that's all they are – just 'off' days. Reassure your child that he's doing well and continue to find 'evidence' that will support the notion that things are changing for the better.

NOTES

ACKNOWLEDGEMENTS

The ideas and techniques used in this book are based on the principles of NLP co-created by **Richard Bandler** and I thank him for giving me his approval to develop this programme.

A big thank you to **Paul McKenna** for his support and for giving me the opportunity to watch and learn so much from him over the years.

I'd also like to thank **Michael Neill** for showing me how "success can be easy". **Mark Hayley, Gabe Guerrero** and **Eric Robbie** – thank you for putting the polish on my NLP skills.

Thanks also to **Bob Gibson** of Staunch for the cover design; **Brian Hubbard** of Studio 86 Photography and Imogen McGuinness for the illustrations.

My children – **George, Tom** and **Clementine** – for simply being the best kids.

And to my partner **Neil** – for his expertise in turning ideas into reality.

USEFUL CONTACT DETAILS

Alicia Eaton – appointments, books and CDs

www.aliciaeaton.co.uk

www.stopbedwettingin7days.co.uk

The General Hypnotherapy Standards Council – Register of qualified Hypnotherapists

www.general-hypnotherapy-register.com

The Society of NLP

www.purenlp.com

The Montessori Society

www.montessori-uk.org

ERIC – Education and Resources for Improving Childhood Continence

www.eric.org.uk